The Basics

of

HOSPICE CHAPLAIN MINISTRY

Practical Help for the New Chaplain

The Basics of
HOSPICE CHAPLAIN MINISTRY

Practical Help for the New Chaplain

John M. Casto

Hisway
Prayer Publication
P.O. Box 762
Jamul, CA 91935

Hospice Chaplain Ministry

Practical Help for the New Chaplain

ISBN-978-1-879545-08-3

Copyright © 2019 by John Casto

All rights reserved

Printed in the United States of America

Published by Hisway Prayer Publications

P. O. Box 762

Jamul, CA 91935

Unless otherwise indicated, all Scripture quotations are taken from the New International Version, of the Bible, Copyright © 1978 by New York International Bible Society. Used by permission. All quotations from the Amplified Bible, Expanded Edition are marked AMP: The Zondervan Corporation and Lockman Foundation 1987. Used by permission. All quotations from the New King James Version Bible are marked NKJV. Thomas Nelson 1982. Used by permission. All quotations from The Living Bible Paraphrased Reference Edition are marked TLB. Tyndale House Publishers 1980.Used by permission.

Dedication

To my wife and best friend for eternity

"A friend knows the song in your heart
And can sing it back to you
When you have forgotten the words."

C. S. Lewis

Foreword

Over the last several years, I have been asked numerous times, "What can a person who is interested in chaplaincy read?" It seems not much is available, especially in the area of hospice.

John started his journey in my Unit 3 class desiring to find what God had for him in chaplaincy. I was John's instructor and suggested he contact a clinical facility near his place of ministry to ask if they could use a volunteer chaplain. This would give him the clinical hours he needed for the course. I felt sure they would see his ability and offer him a job.

In this book, he has written his story for the glory of God, God's call on him and for the benefit of those who are also seeking God's direction. Since that first Unit 3 course, I have seen this take place several times in the lives of other chaplains. What John has written in this book is not only his story but a path of encouragement, hope, and perseverance for those who read it and are looking for the Lord's guidance. The path to chaplaincy is ever-changing as recognition by the "care/clinical industry" grows in what spiritual care brings as a benefit to those being served. What this book describes is not just a path but a reminder that while the path seems difficult, it can be reached.

The joy John brings to those he serves will be part of the praise given someday around the throne of God. Until then, it is my hope that those who read this book will grasp the ability to follow the Lord's leading in their lives.

I am grateful I now have a wonderful tool to give to those who ask, "What can I read about chaplaincy?" My heartfelt congratulations to John and Kathy Casto for the completion of this project. May God bless them and their desire to follow His direction along the path leading John to serve in hospice. Although we chaplains serve, it is often our spouses who are our strength as they live the life of Christ in caring for us.

Rev. Thomas Franklin MPS, BCC, BCCS serves as a Supervisor in CPE for the ICPT online program and as Adjunct Professor for online CPE in the Chaplaincy Program of Crown College. He entered chaplaincy after 34 years of ministry as a Senior Pastor as well as eight years of service in the USAF.

Table of Contents

Introduction

My entry into the chaplaincy began after more than 40 years of ministry — seventeen of which I spent serving as a senior pastor in San Diego. Like every other transition I have experienced, my new direction was confirmed through much prayer and the Word of God.

I was going through my clinical pastoral education to become a certified chaplain. In my fourth unit of training, I needed 400 clinical hours of supervised involvement at a hospital, church or hospice, so I volunteered at Sonata Hospice in San Diego when about 35 patients were there. At the time, in all honesty, I knew very little about hospice or its function. What I did know about hospice, I learned from a hospice chaplain I met while going through Clinical Pastoral Education (CPE). He had been a hospice chaplain for ten years and was prepping to become a chaplain at the Veterans Administration. Needless to say, he inspired me to check out the opportunities that hospice ministry offered.

I had interviewed at one of the local hospitals to volunteer as a chaplain's assistant. However, that entire routine of going door to door, floor by floor, bored me to tears. With due respect for the lead chaplain, I told him it was not a good fit for me. However, it is amazing how God leads us to the exact place we should be. Thank God the lead chaplain was a great mentor.

At Sonata Hospice, I found myself in a completely different environment from a church or hospital. It seemed I was in constant motion from one location to another. I would visit one patient, then off again to see two patients at a different facility. In the middle of visits, I sometimes had to officiate a memorial and then head back to the office to chart. Wow! What an exciting day! But — what was charting?

All the activities, interactions with different patients, and ministry opportunities were actually a perfect fit for John Casto, the "busy bee." At the end of the day, I found myself inspired and very fulfilled. What a godsend! That day, I "knew in my knower" I had discovered God's assignment for me — hospice ministry at Sonata, San Diego.

What is hospice ministry? In most cases, if not all, hospice care is a secular for-profit business. However, I use the word "ministry" instead of work, role, vocation or job for the sake of keeping in the forefront of our minds that everything we do is ministry-related. We are representatives of God, offering His loving care to His creation. *"Whatever you do, work at it with all your heart, as working for the Lord"* (Colossians 3:23, NIV).

I have been a hospice chaplain now for four years with an average of 50 to 60 patients assigned to me monthly, and I still call it hospice ministry. Our agency has a total of 120-130 patients. It is a blessing to be on the team of such a notable agency. As in all businesses, churches, and other organizations, everything rises and falls because of leadership. In our agency, we have great leadership from the corporate level to the field team.

That being said, as I was completing my studies for my Masters of Divinity program and considered what to write for my thesis, I reflected on those early days on staff at a relatively new hospice agency. During that time it was very challenging to source information on how to be a hospice chaplain. I searched for writings related to chaplaincy and specifically, the role of a hospice chaplain but very little was available. Not a lot of informative books had been written on the subject of chaplaincy in general. Most of the basic information I acquired at that time pertained to hospital chaplaincy. It was relatively easy to find practical information about first responder, fire department, and military chaplains. Nearly everywhere people meet or work, you find the ministry of the chaplain and plenty of good information about these ministries. However, for whatever reason, there was a void of practical information about the hospice chaplain' ministry.

Recognizing the need, I was inspired to write this book about the ministry of hospice chaplains — who they are, what they do, and where they work. It offers practical help for the new hospice chaplain, the inquiring chaplain with an interest in this ministry, and perhaps a pastor who feels God may lead him or her in this direction.

My objective is to provide you with the basic information I desired about this ministry but could not find. My ultimate goal has become a reality. Hopefully, this book will help you the new hospice chaplain or young minister find your way in this complicated world.

Chapter One
The Call of God

First of all, I want to help clarify the call of God in your life and specifically, the call into hospice ministry. Anyone who has been in ministry very long at all knows God has an appointed time and place of ministry for them. We find this assurance in the book of Acts: *"He determines the exact times set for them and the exact places they should live. God did this so that men would seek him and perhaps reach out for Him and find Him, though he is not far from each of us. For in Him we live and move and have our being"* (Acts 17:26-28, NIV). God has gifted each of us with the tools to complete our own assignments. Our gifts will open the doors for us. Hence, we don't just try to find a job. We seek God and discover our ministries.

The ministry of the hospice chaplain is as much a call of God as any specific area of Christian service. Indeed,

God calls us to specific areas of ministry: pastor, youth pastor, worship leader, hospital minister, hospice minister, prison minister, etc. How else would there be any passion and determination to weather the challenges these ministries bring with them? Just as God called Abraham to get up and "Go to a land I will show you," He calls us to specific places (Acts 17:26, NIV). "He anoints us ...to bind up the broken hearted... set at liberty them that are captive... preach the year of the Lord" (Luke 4:18, KJV). The call of God, hearing the voice of God, and the confirmation of God's hand on our lives bring the fulfillment and fruit we bear. As hospice chaplains, we see the fruit of God's hand on our lives continually.

We should all keep in mind that ministry to the sick is a privilege. We must have a sincere desire to support and comfort ill patients, bring hope and encourage faith: "I was sick and you visited me" (Matthew 25:36, NIV).

I remember making a hospice visit on a cold, rainy day after having a long day of ministry the day before and a short night of rest. I wasn't feeling very well but my first patient of the day put things into perspective. The patient had hearing challenges so another patient nearby named Kathryn offered assistance. She got very close to the patient's ear and repeated words of encouragement of God's love and forgiveness to her.

6

The patient received Christ's forgiveness. I made the same appeal to Kathryn because she had quoted the same scriptures and prayed the same prayer. She gladly received the Lord as well. I was thrilled, to say the least, and remarked, "Wow, look what God set up today." With a smile, Kathryn said, "God may have set this up today — but John — you came to visit us." That visit still inspires me to this day.

In the book, *The Work of the Chaplain*, the authors make an important statement:

The chaplain is called to minister to the disenfranchised of society. This group of people includes the homeless, disabled, terminally ill, the uneducated and the learned, as well as those without shoes, the 'well heeled,' those with 'white collars, blue collars, and those with no shirt at all. The list is almost endless because of multiplied varying types and groups of people in the world. Nevertheless, God has raised up chaplains to reach out to them.[1]

They also said, "*The call to chaplain ministry is a unique call, which is preceded by a clear call to vocational service in spiritual care.*"[2] This statement is in line with what I have found to be true in seeking God's will in my own life. As I previously stated, the scripture that always brought me comfort, confirming the direction of my life is found in Acts 17:26 (NIV), "*He determines the exact places where we should live and move and have our being.*"

Although I thought I was only going to volunteer for a few hours a week at a hospice company to comply with the requirements of CPE training, I found within days that hospice ministry was the *exact* ministry for me. I no longer desired — or even considered — a position in a hospital, emergency ward or anywhere else. I found *the place* where I was supposed to "*live and move and have my being.*"

God will lead the easiest way we will follow. Sometimes that particular leading comes by a scripture that stands out in our daily reading or a comment by someone who gets our attention. When Kathy and I moved with our two teenage daughters from Dallas to San Diego, we needed to find a home where our girls could attend the recommended school district. On the plane ride to San Diego, Kathy noticed a colorful brochure stuffed into the back pocket of the seat in front of her. Before we exited the plane, she picked up the brochure, showed it to me, and said, "I don't know what this means, but these words have been leaping out to me every time I look at this: 'Jump on this one.'"

We spent the entire two days looking at homes in the areas zoned for the girls' schools and had not located anything we could afford. We were exhausted and disappointed, to say the least. It was Sunday evening, and we had our bags packed to catch our flight back to Dallas the next morning when the phone rang. The owner of one of the houses we had tried to visit was on the line. He explained he had been out of town and had just received our message that we wanted to look at his house for rent. The house was still available, and we could see it the next morning.

With an afternoon flight, that worked for us, so we had some hope we might find something. When we drove to the house, it seemed like we drove forever into the foothills. We finally arrived in the quiet, picturesque neighborhood, and our hearts lifted. The home met all the requirements for the school area. However, the lease was a little more than our budget. We hesitated, but the Holy Spirit brought back the words on the brochure vividly: "Jump on this one!"

Did we take that as a directive from the Holy Spirit? Absolutely! We even missed our flight that day to pay the deposit and sign the lease. In all the years we leased the home, the owner never raised the rent. In addition, as Kathy was praying about purchasing the home, she heard these words in her spirit: "Wait for the dip." Although that message was peculiar, we knew it was a directive from the Holy Spirit and exactly what it meant. There was going to be an economic downturn, which would cause the housing market to fall tremendously. We were to wait for that event to purchase the home at a drastically reduced price — in California that could mean thousands of dollars.

Previously, we had approached the owner at various times to purchase the home; he assured us he would never sell the property. He considered it part of his estate. However, with clear instructions in prayer to "Wait for the dip," we decided to take action on the Spirit's word and prepare for the purchase of the home. We would have to be debt-free. We sold everything we had accumulated that was not "bolted down" in our garage, and we saved every windfall profit from any source. We paid off everything –credit cards and cars – and learned to live on a cash basis.

Ten years later, a major economic crash occurred in our nation, which caused the real estate market to fall. That same year, the owner passed away. In his will, he stated that the lessees had the first option to buy his homes. We were able to purchase the home at the much-reduced price with no down payment and equity in the home. There is a God in heaven!

I share these stories to show God will speak to us and lead us anyway we will *listen and obey Him!* He has a perfect will for our lives if we will allow the Holy Spirit to walk with us daily. Following God and doing His will have always proven to be challenging. In a lot of cases, Kathy and I have found that doing God's will has been "traveling the road less traveled."[3] Why? It keeps us holding on to God's hand. "Life never gets easier. We get stronger."[4] However, one word from God allows you to run into an unknown future with a smile.

As I briefly mentioned in the introduction, there was a time when I was between points "A" and "B" trying to find the will of God for my life. I had recently resigned my position as senior pastor of the church my wife and I had founded and served as pastors for 16 years. I had just started my fourth unit of Clinical Pastoral Education. I was also not settled on what area of ministry I wanted to focus on as a chaplain. Admittedly, it was beginning to frustrate me because I knew I had a "general" call of God to be a chaplain but that was not specific enough for me. I wanted to know exactly where God was calling me.

I seriously considered becoming a veteran's or emergency care chaplain. However, as I moved through CPE, read job descriptions, interviewed chaplains, and prayed, those avenues fell "flat" in my spirit. Nothing about those vocations inspired me. I was disillusioned until I volunteered with the hospice agency. There, I received the clarification we had been praying for. I found my place of ministry.

Interestingly, in my pastoral ministry of over 40 years, I preached a lot of sermons, but I only shared my testimony once or twice. Why? After everybody there heard it, unfortunately, it was "old news." However, in the last five years as a hospice chaplain, I have shared my story/testimony hundreds of times and the fruit is eternal. Multiple souls have been won to the Lord through the remarkable story of my salvation, deliverance from Vietnam, and subsequent drug addiction. The point I am making is that in hospice ministry, the Holy Spirit leads us to many opportunities, not only to share the love of Christ but to also tell our personal stories of salvation.

Every one of us has been given a story to tell and a song to sing. It's all about the day we met the Lord. "*I waited patiently for the LORD; he turned to me and heard my cry. He lifted me out of the slimy pit, out of the mud and*

12

*mire; he set my feet on a rock and gave me a firm place to stand. He put a **new song in my mouth**, a hymn of praise to our God. **Many will see** and fear the* LORD *and **put their trust in him**"* (Psalm 40:1-3, NIV) [Emphasis mine].

God has fulfilled those scriptures in my life, not only in pastoral ministry but more so in hospice ministry as a chaplain. I will share my story at this time as an example of what God has led me to use as a tool of ministry.

Notes:

1. Paget and McCormack, *The Work of the Chaplain,* p 5.

2. Ibid p 118.

3. Peck, M. Scott, M.D. *The Road Less Traveled: A New Psychology of Love, Traditional Values and Spiritual Growth* p 312.

4. Author Unknown.

Chapter Two
My Story

I was the second child born into a military family of five children: three boys and two girls. Wallace Casto, my dad, and his parents were of Choctaw Indian descent. My mom Mildred's parents were German. Dad had no religious background. Mom was a Baptist. The only time we ever attended church as a family was at weddings and funerals – mostly funerals.

My dad fought in both World War II and the Korean wars. No doubt those horrific experiences influenced his alcohol addiction and the family abuse we endured through my school years. He retired after twenty years in the military and drifted from job to job. The verbal and physical abuse continued until all of us finally left home after graduating from high school.

My learning challenges came to light in the seventh grade. Actually, I struggled all through school and into college. Years later, I was diagnosed with dyslexia. With a few vitamins, diet adjustments, and coping skills, I have been able to successfully progress in my life and ministry.

It was September 1970, while I was on leave, en route to Vietnam that I met a beautiful young lady in Paris, Arkansas. She was a senior in high school and a classmate of my sister. I was twenty, handsome, bulletproof, and arrogant, but I was humble about it. Unbeknownst to me, one date I had with Kathy would impact my life for eternity.

Kathy was the first born-again Christian I had ever met up close and personal. We had a wonderful date at the movies that evening. She promised she and her church would be praying for me. That was a surprise because, at that time, no one had ever offered to pray for me. After that evening, my encounters with God started.

Two days later, I said goodbye to family and friends. I was on a plane to Cam Ranh Bay, South Vietnam. Upon arriving, I was assigned to the 173rd Airborne Division. Six weeks later, while on patrol, one of our men tripped an explosive device that badly wounded three of us. By the grace of God, I lived through that situation and was transferred back to the United States. Unfortunately, the two other soldiers did not survive. After six months of recovery, I was honorably discharged from the army. I returned to Paris, Arkansas and, of course, one of the first people I was excited to see was that beautiful, young lady I had met months before.

Kathy and I began a dating relationship that always included attending church. Unfortunately, I had continued the drug use that began in Vietnam. That lifestyle continued for the next year and a half and our relationship eventually fell apart. Kathy's relationship with God had diminished and mine had never really started. Thankfully, she and her church continued to pray for me.

Within a week of our breakup, God supernaturally intervened in my life. I will spare the details but share with you the most important thing. Through a chain of events, I felt like the second coming of Jesus Christ had taken place, and I had been left behind. Talk about an epiphany! Wow! That surely was one for me.

I experienced a radical change in my heart and lifestyle. In the following months, my life and decisions became Christ-centered. Life-changing events began to happen quickly. Miraculously, I was born again, which means *"Old things are passed away; behold, all things are become new"* (2 Corinthians 5:17, KJV).

Kathy and I were married six weeks later on June 30th. A month after our wedding, I felt called into the ministry. After counsel with our pastor, family, and friends, we both enrolled at Southwestern Assemblies of God University in Waxahachie, Texas. We graduated together and began our journey in ministry. At the time of this writing, we had just celebrated our 47th wedding anniversary.

That is a condensed version of my story, which is always good news. It creates opportunities to share when patients ask religious or spiritual questions at various times in my work week. The Holy Spirit usually prompts me if the situation is appropriate and the timing is right. It is amazing how God uses our stories of salvation, deliverance, and healing to change the lives of those on the brink of eternity. The longer I work in hospice ministry, the more I learn most people are closer to the kingdom of God than we think.

Chapter Three
The History of Hospice Ministry

Most people have a general idea about hospice ministry; however, few of us have any idea of its history and how it has evolved to its present function. This historical review provides very important information for the new chaplain, anyone working in hospice, and those trying to discover the will of God for their lives. I have to confess in all my years of ministry as a pastor making hospital visits and officiating funerals, I had never heard the term hospice chaplain ever used.

The first information I received about hospice care came by way of meeting a hospice chaplain during my CPE training. He had served in that role for ten years and his company required him to take at least two units of CPE. As we interacted throughout our training, I began to get glimpses of his ministry to people during their transition at the end of life. I realized I knew absolutely nothing about this ministry opportunity; yet, I felt the Holy Spirit drawing me in this direction.

Admittedly, I volunteered at the hospice company for many reasons but mostly to fulfill the requirements of my CPE studies. During this time I began a self-study of the history of hospice ministry. It wasn't long before I discovered that hospice ministry had become a hospice business. In most cases today, ministry is not a place. Rather, it is contained within the person of the chaplain, minister or any other God-called individual working as a doctor, nurse, administrator, etc. What started out historically as communities of care operated by like-minded caregivers have gone through 2,000-plus years of transformation. From "The Good Samaritan" in Luke 10:25-27, workhouses of human neglect in England during the Age of Enlightenment in the 18th century to communities of care for AIDS victims in the 1980s to the present – hospice has developed into a very lucrative business.

Our modern term "hospice" comes from the Latin word, hospes, meaning both host and guest, and symbolizing the mutual caring of people for one another. We get our word "hospitality" from this root word, and it refers to a place of shelter and rest. It can be traced back to medieval times [and further back, in my opinion], when it referred to a place of shelter and rest for weary or ill travelers on a long journey. (Wikipedia)

It's no stretch of the imagination to see that, no doubt, those references of *"places of shelter and rest for weary or ill travelers"* were inspired by passages found in the Bible. The apostle Peter exhorts us to *"practice hospitality"* (1 Peter 4:9, AMP). The word "hospice" is derived from the word "hospitality." In this Amplified Bible Version key elements of hospice care from Christian values are seen in this scripture.

Practice <u>hospitality</u> to one another (those of the household of faith). [Be <u>hospitable</u>, be <u>a lover of strangers</u>, with <u>brotherly affection</u> for the <u>unknown guests</u>, <u>the foreigners</u>, <u>the poor</u>, and <u>all others</u> who come your way who are of Christ's body.] And [in each instance] <u>do it ungrudgingly</u> (<u>cordially and graciously</u>, without <u>complaining</u> but as representing Him). (1 Peter 4:9, AMP)

Those same values are also applied in the parable of the Good Samaritan, taught by Jesus, who embodies the hospice philosophy of love and care:

He went to him and bandaged his wounds, pouring on oil and wine. Then he put the man on his own donkey, took him to an inn and took care of him. The next day he took out two silver coins and gave them to the innkeeper. 'Look after him,' he said, 'and when I return, I will

reimburse you for any extra expense you may have.
(Luke 10:30-35, NIV)

In these scriptures, we notice two hospice concepts: "Love thy Neighbor," "Care for Those in Need," and an exhortation by our Lord to *"Go do likewise"* (Luke 10:37, NIV). These and other scriptures no doubt inspired believers to be their brothers' keepers, to provide care for the annual travelers who converged on Jerusalem every year for the Passover and other religious celebrations, as well as those journeying to other locations. It is easy to conceive that these places of shelter would naturally spring up all along the main routes of travel to care for and give rest to the weary.

The early development of these concepts and application for caring originated in the 11th century with the Roman Catholic Church. Their focus was on chronically and terminally ill care. Hospice care continued here and there in different countries for centuries with little notoriety until the mid-1800s. Florence Nightingale, who gave up her Victorian wealth to care for the dying, and Elisabeth Fry, an English Quaker with the Sisters of Charity, were champions of the suffering. They made dramatic contributions to the growth of this ministry. *"The Sisters of Charity developed a shelter in Dublin, Ireland in 1910 for 'the incurably ill' and called it in English 'a hospice.'"* 1

The modern-day concept of hospice care was pioneered by Dame Cicely Saunders who opened St. Christopher's Hospice in London, England, in 1967. Saunders actually introduced the concept of palliative care, which focuses on the comfort of the patient through pain management rather than treating for a cure.

It was interesting to see how God used Dame Saunders' own chronic health issues to lead her into medical social work where she developed a relationship with a dying refugee. Out of that relationship, she formed her direction and philosophy for caring for terminally ill patients. She felt the patient should be cared for with compassion regarding their fears and concerns. She introduced the concept of focusing on the patient rather than the disease. Soon, she also developed the technique of pain control and total care for dying patients that has become the cornerstone of hospices all over the world.

Her ideas on "total pain" addressed comforting the patient psychologically and spiritually, as well as physically. *"Her initial goal of relieving the pain of cancer patients had grown to embrace dying patients all over the world. She was also aware that she had changed the face of medicine forever."* [2] This woman's ideas pushed the mindset of that time to a different understanding of palliative care in this area. She is credited with establishing the first modern-day hospice with specialized care for dying patients in London, England. It still functions to this day.

It seems that hospice care has come full circle. Ms. Saunders was a very caring person who was drawn to people in pain. Today, the new buzzword is "patient-centered care." Those words relate well to Ms. Saunders' work. *"It was through caring for them that she came to understand the diversity of their needs, then to see a pattern in that diversity; it was through her involvement with her patients that she found the stimulus for the work she was to undertake ... she learnt from the dying in order to help the dying."* 3

In 1969, Elisabeth Kubler-Ross wrote the book *Death and Dying,* which helped start the hospice movement in the United States. Kubler-Ross was instrumental in getting Congress to pass the Medicare Hospice Benefit, which made hospice care available through a Medicare benefit.

The need for hospice care was greatly increased in the US beginning in the mid-1980s. At the time, we all remember what was called the AIDS epidemic. It was a time of tragic misunderstanding of the disease and great fear. Unfortunately, many people during that period were inhumane to those with the disease because of fear and misinformation. However *"the hospice movement came along just in time to show us how to care for people with AIDS."*[4] In 1984, David Kessler wrote the following in the *Needs of the Dying*: *"I thought of hospice as a physical location, a facility where the terminally ill were cared for... through my work as a nurse I came to realize that hospice is a philosophy - a way of caring for loved ones."*[5]

During that time, staff members at hospitals were uncomfortable working with people with AIDS. Thus, the home became the place for the dying. Kessler created one of the first companies that offered services to terminally ill patients; the majority were AIDS and cancer patients. This was a wonderful example of humanity caring for humanity.

Barbara Karnes, author of *The Final Act of Living* made a similar discovery about hospice around the same time Kessler did. She became disillusioned with nursing soon after graduating from nursing school and made a life-changing discovery. She writes:

The hospice concept was everything I thought nursing was going to be. It was holistic. It involved all parts of a person – not just the physical, but emotional, mental, and even spiritual. It included the family and significant others. It avoided medical procedures whenever possible. It dealt in comfort and quality and most of all personhood. The hospice concept focused on people who happened to have a disease, not on a disease that had a person. 6

Today, hospice is a vital part of our society and culture. It is a tremendous opportunity to express the love, grace, and forgiveness of our Lord and Savior. I thank God for all those who have made life-changing contributions throughout history to bring us to this point in time.

The whole philosophy of hospice ministry is to develop a team of caring people who offer patient-centered care. I am honored God has placed me in a team that truly cares for patients' end-of-life journey.

Notes:

1. Stoddard, Sandal The Hospice Movement: *A Better Way of Caring for the Dying* p 80.

2. Boulay, Shirley du. Updated by Rankin, Marianne. Cicely Saunders: *The Founder of the Modern Hospice Movement Introduction.*

3. Ibid p 50.

4. Stoddard, Sandal The Hospice Movement: *A Better Way of Caring for the Dying* p 264.

5. Kessler, David *The Needs of the Dying* p xvii.

6. Karnes, Barbara *The Final Act of Living* p 3.

Chapter Four
Spirit-Led Ministry

We have talked about the call of God, as well as its importance in the chaplain's life and ministry. Being led by the Holy Spirit on a daily basis is in that same category of importance.

To become a certified chaplain a high level of education is required. It is also necessary to be exposed to various psychological counseling methods and techniques. However, let us not forget that as born-again believers, we must depend upon the Holy Spirit. In my opinion, through the years from Anton Boisen to present, some CPE training programs have unwisely focused more on the psychological training and counseling techniques to the exclusion of ministry.

I recommend a good book *Where God Comes In - The Divine "Plus" in Counseling* written by William E. Crane a seasoned pastor and counselor. It puts everything into perspective. He writes:

> *There are five types of experiences which provide, in varying degrees, the deeper self-encounter which accelerates the counselors' growth: personal psychotherapy, clinical pastoral training, supervision of one's counseling, sensitivity training groups, and reality-practice."* Pastor Crane continues, *"Although these five experiences are comprehensive, I feel that more emphasis should be given to one aspect of training which every pastor has access to - <u>an awareness of and dependence upon the Holy Spirit as the Wonderful Counselor</u>.*[1]

The pastor reiterates this point later writing, *"If we are not guided and controlled by this Spirit of God, we are to a large degree incapacitated, limited to dealing with our counselees on the superficial level and avoiding their spiritual needs."*[2] Thank you Pastor Crane.

Learning psychological methods is helpful but limited in use and man's best effort to fix/heal himself apart from God. Most of the psychological theories were birthed during the industrial age when *man* thought of himself as "Mister Wonderful." Humanism developed. Intellectualism raised its head. All was created for man and God was excluded. How sad.

That being said, if you are a new or inquiring hospice chaplain, everything you learn in CPE will be life-changing and helpful. All the education and training you acquire can become tools in the hands of the Holy Spirit. He truly is a gift from our heavenly Father. Jesus said, "*I will pray to the father and He will give you another Comforter that will abide with you forever*" (John 14:16 NIV). He is our helper and guide. He speaks to and through us to bring life and light to whomever He leads us. God in heaven lives and moves on the earth in the person of the Holy Spirit. "*For the eyes of the Lord run to and fro throughout the whole earth, to show himself strong on behalf of those whose heart is perfect toward him*" (2 Chronicles 16:9, NKJ).

As hospice chaplains, we have been given one of the greatest opportunities for ministry a person can imagine. However, let me caution you. When I say ministry, I am not talking about some door-to-door witnessing or evangelistic program. I am talking about daily walking out your journey, expressing the love of a caring God. In the words of Saint Francis of Assisi, "*Preach the gospel at all times and when necessary ... use words.*"3 As chaplains, we choose to walk along the same path as the patients. When the Holy Spirit gives opportunity, we offer the love of God in word and deed.

However, there are days when we have divine appointments. For example, I had one a morning walking down the hall in a skilled nursing facility. I noticed a man sitting in his wheelchair as I turned into the nurses' station to pick up some patient information. Then I heard someone behind me say, *"Hey, what are you doing back there?"*

I turned around with a smile and said, *"I'm a chaplain; I'm allowed back here."*

"You're a chaplain? You look like a doctor," the old gentleman responded.

Smiling, I replied, *"I'm sorry. I get accused of that all the time. How can I help you?"*

He asked, *"If you're a chaplain, will you pray for me?"*

"I can. What would you like for me to pray about?" I inquired.

With a brief conversation, I found he needed prayer for his business. I also learned he had drifted away from God and wanted to come back. I prayed for his business, led him in a prayer of repentance, and welcomed him back home. As I turned around, another elderly man was standing with his walker. He said he had overheard everything and asked for prayer. I had the same conversation I had with the first gentleman and learned he, too, had drifted away from the Lord and wanted to return. It was so touching. He removed the hat he was wearing out of respect, asked for forgiveness, and declared, "Jesus is Lord!" If there were any nurses in the station at the time, it might have caught them by surprise. Our God is a good God!

You have to keep in mind that in all of the stories I share, these precious people were in hospice care and had less than six months to live. Some of my patients have weeks, others only days. I have sat and held the hands of those who only had hours. The comforting news is that the Holy Spirit is always at work, and we learn to be patient.

One patient of mine, who reported to be of a certain religious persuasion, told me not to try to proselytize him and to leave him alone. I chose to offer friendship and greeted him on each visit, but I would never bring up the subject of religion unless he mentioned something. One morning, I woke up with the feeling I had to go see this man that day. Sadly, he was too medicated for a visit that morning. The next day, the same urgency was in my spirit. When I arrived at the patient's room, as I opened the door to check on him, he immediately welcomed me into the room. I asked him if he remembered who I was.

He responded, *"Oh, yes, you are the chaplain,"* and he extended his hand to shake mine. *"I'm so glad to see you,"* he added.

I asked, *"How can I help you today?"*

He began to grieve over his life and how many things he had done wrong, I encouraged him that was in the past and asked him what he wanted to do about the future.

"I don't know Chaplain," he replied.

I asked if he would mind if I read some scriptures. To my surprise, he did not object. As I read the 23rd Psalm, he started quoting it with me. I slowly read *The Lord's Prayer*, and he quoted that as well. I paused and asked, *"Do you know what you just did?"*

He paused as well, and said, *"I think I just asked for forgiveness."*

I affirmed his statement saying, *"Yes, you did, and God heard your prayer."*

Then, he cried out to God loudly, *"Oh, God, Oh, God; Oh God, forgive me!"* (Wow, look at our God!) After prayer, he was calm and peaceful. I asked where he learned those scriptures.

He said, *"My grandmother taught me as a child."*

Look at the power of seed sown years ago!

The point here is that any hospital or hospice chaplain must always endeavor to be led by the Spirit of God. We must use wisdom in our application and timing to minister the love of God.

I exhort you as a new chaplain to take the time and read through the Gospel of John chapters 14, 15, and 16 in various translations. While you do that, allow the Holy Spirit to give you a fresh revelation of Himself. He will speak to you in your thoughts, impressions, and spirit. Jesus said He will, *"teach you much, as well as remind you of everything I myself have told you"* (John 14:26, TLB). Chaplains, we have not learned everything; there is much more to learn about God. *"The Sovereign Lord has given me an instructed tongue, to know the word that sustains the weary. He wakens me morning by morning, wakens my ear to listen like one being taught"* (Isaiah 50:4).

The "weary" are all around us in hospice ministry. The Holy Spirit desires to give us directives, insights, impressions and His words to guide us to them. *"Very early in the morning...Jesus got up...and went to a solitary and there He prayed"* (Mark 1:33-35). *"Call unto me I will show you things you do not know"* (Jeremiah 33:3). Let God warm your heart in the morning to speak to a cold and indifferent world about His great love for them.

Remember, we did not choose Him; He chose us to go and bear fruit. The Holy Spirit will tell us where to go and what to do (Galatians 5:16, TLB). Stay close to Him in your quiet time and daily walk. Every day will be a new day for you, your patients, and everyone around you.

Notes:

1. Crane, William E. *Where God Comes In: The Divine "Plus" in Counseling* p 24.

2. Ibid. p 104.

3. Paget, Naomi K. and McCormack, Janet, R. *The Work of the Chaplain* p 117.

Chapter Five
Patient-Centered Care

As mentioned before, the new trend today in healthcare is patient-centered care. It is about providing care to a person with respect, dignity, and compassion. The patient is the primary factor in the care being given. In my opinion, the ministry of the hospice chaplain *is* patient-centered. We take a holistic approach ministering not only to the body but also to the soul and spirit of the patient.

Extensive studies have been made regarding the spiritual care (prayer, scripture reading, and spiritual valves discussions, etc.) that the chaplain provides to the patient. These studies show that the aspects of spiritual care enable the patient to cope better with their end of life challenges. The studies also concluded that the spiritual support chaplains offer the patient is *invaluable.* Imagine that! God says, *"Call to me, and I will answer you, and show you great and mighty things, which you do not know"* (Jeremiah 33:3 NKJV). Thankfully, someone took the time and effort to prove what most of us in ministry discovered experientially. Prayer invites God to do what we can't do in any given situation.

Patient-Centered Care Starts as Soon as You Meet the Patient

As a new chaplain, please note that patient-centered care begins when we first meet the patient to do our assessment. This is the time we allow the patient to tell his or her story. Let them do most of the talking. You are there to gather information, as well as identify the patient's feelings and emotions. You must also learn to listen, not only with your ears but your eyes as well. Facial expressions of pain and different emotions are opportunities for inquiry. I have found the more you listen with focused care, the more open the patient becomes and a level of trust forms. My wife and I have an expression we have used over the years for focused communication. We say to each other, *"I need you to listen with your face."* Both of us know that what we hear next will be very important. Listening is truly a ministry in itself.

I'm learning that the voice of suffering will speak if we listen long enough. Through the patient's "storytelling" process, we discover the patient's history, family dynamics, anxieties, emotional wounds, and health issues. In doing so, we are not only informed to determine a plan of care for treatment, but we have also discovered the patient's spiritual interests to be explored later.

The Patient Is in Control

Patient-centered care basically allows the patients to be in control while they are in our care. They are part of the decision-making process in how we care for them. In our hospice care, each patient is assigned a team that includes a doctor(s), nurse, social worker, home health-aide, music therapist, and a chaplain. An initial care conference is held with the patient or his/her representative. A plan of care with the patient's best interest in mind is outlined, discussed, and implemented. The patient's wants and needs must always stay in our focus.

In our routine visits, the patient is also in control. I always ask permission from the patient to read a scripture, pray or to include him/her in my prayers. The patient should be treated as a living human being, regardless of what stage of end-of-life they may be.

The Needs of the Dying

When I was going through my CPE training, I discovered books that have become very dear to my heart. They have helped me better understand all of the above. *The Needs of the Dying* by David Kessler is highly recommended. It contains the heart's cry of the dying and how we as chaplains can give God's love in a practical way. It should be required reading for all hospice team members.

The following are the needs of the dying that Kessler presents. You can use these for guidance, education, and application for the patients, as well as their family members:

- The need to be treated as a living being

- The need to maintain a sense of hopefulness however changing its focus may be

- The need to be cared for by those who can maintain a sense of hopefulness however changing this maybe

- The need to express feelings and emotions about death in one's own way

- The need to participate in decisions concerning one's care

- The need to be cared for by compassionate, sensitive, and knowledgeable people

- The need for continuing medical care, even though the goals may change from "cure" to "comfort"

- The need to have all questions answered honestly and fully

- The need to seek spirituality

- The need to be free of physical pain

- The need to express feelings and emotions about pain in one's way

- The need for children to participate in the process of death

- The need to understand the process of death

- The need to die in peace and dignity

- The need not to die alone

- The need to know that the sanctity of the body will be respected after death[1]

"Death is an inescapable part of life. We can't prevent it; nor can we prevent the inevitable pain of separation it causes.

However, we can make the experience of death better, both for the living and the dying."[2]

Hospice chaplains are called upon to minister to the needs of the patient. A large part of that is walking with the patient through the dying process. The dying experience is unique to us all. No two deaths are similar and each patient needs help through this part of life. As the hospice chaplain, your role is to make the patient's transition as comfortable as possible in peace and dignity.

Be Familiar with the Process of Death

For the new chaplain to best exemplify patient-centered care he/she has to be familiar with the end of life process. There are no "Dying 101" courses available that I'm aware of. However, I can recommend the works of Barbara Karnes, which are the closest writings to it. Barbara Karnes, RN is an end of life educator who has been contributing to hospice healthcare for over 25 years. All of her booklets are simply written in non-medical terms. This approach is significant because our patients and family members have embarked on a journey of "unknowns." A lot of misinformation about end of life care is out there, which this author can help correct.

The ministry of the chaplain is to comfort, encourage, and when appropriate, educate. Please avail yourself of these tools (bkbooks.com).The greatest example of pastoral and patient-centered care is our Lord and Savior. He came to heal the sick – not the well. He showed compassion, concern, and empathy in all of His dealings with everyone. My prayer is that I will never say no to a cry for help. May my ears always stay in tune spiritually to hear beyond their words and expressions of concern, so I can find the best path to minister the love of God.

Notes:

1. Kessler, David *The Needs of the Dying* p xi.

2. Ibid p xix.

Chapter Six
Ministry Preparation

We have talked about the call of God, history, and being led by the Spirit. Now, we will take a look at ministry preparation. This is very important to becoming a board-certified chaplain. Although you may find a place of ministry as a chaplain before finishing your course, most organizations will require you to continue studying until you get your certification. I will address each of these requirements but not in any particular order of importance. I will also attempt to keep you encouraged.

Again, I emphasize the need to know God has called you to be a chaplain – and specifically, a hospice chaplain. This is extremely important because CPE training requires an investment and presents similar challenges as pursuing any college or seminary education. However, Kathy and I have learned that where *God guides, He provides*. Also, if it is *God's will, it is His bill*. Let me quickly add that those are not just platitudes or wishful thinking. Our lives today are a testimony of God's provision. We watched God miraculously provide the cost of each of the four units of CPE, the expenses involved for board certification, attendance to the corresponding annual conference, the completion of my Master of Divinity, and in so many other ways as well.

Theological Training

Education is a very important step in becoming a board-certified chaplain, which is a very advantageous goal. As far as employment is concerned, you can be hired while working on a master's degree and CPE training. I was blessed to be able to do both and be employed with a hospice agency at the same time. However, I already had 40-plus years of pastoral experience, which helped tremendously. As we start our God-directed journey toward chaplaincy, we will find God's favor working on our behalf.

Perhaps you already have your Master of Arts or Master of Divinity and are exploring the possibility of hospice ministry. Maybe you are at a different stage of

Ministry Preparation

education needing to complete your bachelor's degree or your master's programs. Whatever the case, you can study online. Online distance-learning schools have become good options for those who cannot commute/move to a seminary campus or who have family/job responsibilities that make it impossible to attend classes on campus.

Although I took courses through the years towards my master's program here in San Diego at a local seminary, I never completed my studies. Thank God, a dear pastor friend of mine suggested that I check out Jacksonville Theological Seminary. He said it was an online distance-learning school that offered, not only Masters and Master of Divinity degrees, but doctoral degrees as well.

I took his advice and discovered that the seminary exceeded my greatest expectations. I was able to complete my Master of Divinity degree and my wife Kathy completed her Master in Christian Counseling. The online distance-learning program was an excellent option for us at this season of our lives.

If you are looking for a ministry-focused degree program that offers practical courses in these fields of ministry: Bible theology, counseling, teaching, worship, chaplaincy, and much more, I highly recommend this seminary. It is affordable and you can learn at your pace.

Earning a degree from Jacksonville Theological Seminary (JTS) is no different from any other graduate-level educational program. However, one of the advantages of the online program is that you can start the courses you need immediately instead of waiting for the next semester or year to begin.

Clinical Pastoral Education - 4 Units

The following requirements are for board certification. If you have been looking online for a chaplain's position lately, I'm sure you may have noticed that in most cases, you need at least two units of CPE to be hired. Why is certification important? It recognizes your competence, helps you do an efficient job, and essentially shows a level of commitment. Like other organizations, hospices that fail to employ qualified people to care for patients could face serious consequences. Certification sets the standard of care employees are expected to provide. It is also critical for hospice care providers to document and maintain the professional experience of their staff.

Let me share a little word of wisdom to emphasize the importance of taking this training. I have been with the same hospice agency for the last four years. Like any other business venture, most hospices fail within the first two years. In America, the hospice companies that make it beyond the two-year mark are reimbursed by Medicare and come under the scrutiny of our federal government.

Our hospice agency has successfully gone through at least two lower-level audits. But then there is (drum roll, please) the Joint Commission audit. That name sounds a little scary just reading it. Well, they do give offices a week or so warning, but it's even scarier to have them show up in the office and go through everything: patient records, visits made by the entire team, licenses, RNs (Registered Nurses), CHHAs (Certified Home Health Aides), MSWs (Medical Social Workers), chaplains' ordinations, financials, etc. Just name it, and they want to look at it in the office and out in the field as well. It is a very stressful situation to have these wonderful people stay with the office team for seven full days. Therefore, it is an enormous accomplishment when a hospice successfully passes the audit as our Sonata Hospice has done consistently.

Our hospice agency is good to go for the next three years. All the preparations I have suggested you make are required by the Joint Commission for every organization that employs chaplains. So the time to get busy is now.

For CPE training, I recommend you enroll in an accredited online long-distance training program. I suggest the Institute of Clinical Pastoral Training (*https://clinicalpastoraled.org/*). When I first heard about this program five years ago, I could not believe it. It was too good to be true! I was very skeptical because of the opposition I encountered in San Diego. I had sent my application and resume to three different organizations that offered CPE training in the city. I was declined entry to their programs. They either misplaced my application and resume or the program was suddenly full. Moreover, they informed me they did not know when the next CPE unit would be available.

Be that as it may, *"All things work together for good to those who love God and are the called according to His purpose"* (Romans 8:28 NIV). Those events stole my hope for CPE training temporarily until a friend recommended the above-mentioned institute for clinical training. God always leads us the easiest way we will follow.

The Association of Certified Christian Chaplains (ACCC), which I joined over five years ago, is one I also endorse. I not only received my four units of CPE, but I also got my board certification from ACCC.

Application can be made online at certifiedchaplains.org to enroll in the Institute of Clinical Pastoral Training section.

Again, I wish I could have found the help and information I am excited to share with you. As you read further, I will provide a quick overview of the training I experienced, with some explanation and further recommendations.

When I called Certified Christian Chaplains, I knew it required four units to become a board-certified chaplain. Unfortunately, I did not have a hospice chaplain to guide or mentor me through this process. In fact, the chaplain who encouraged me to inquire about this new training had only heard about it himself. He neither did it nor completed his master's degree. He had been on staff for five years at a large hospital here in San Diego as the emergency room chaplain. I wondered how a steady diet of that would affect a person.

Interesting to note is that was six years ago when there was little to no interest in CPE programs.

However, just last January, the Institute of Clinical Pastoral Training received its accreditation from the U.S. Department of Education.

The online program is an excellent way to complete CPE training. You will need to determine how much you can afford and how much time you can invest. A lot of chaplains I have known only complete the required two units and immediately go job hunting. If you choose that journey, you must always keep in mind that the ultimate goal should be board certification. Big Brother (our government) will be checking in at each hospice company's HR (Human Resources) with questions and eventually, requirements. Get ahead of the curve before HR asks for a copy of the CPE units you completed. It was a good feeling when they asked for mine, and I was the only one out of the three chaplains who had done all the required units.

Summary and Breakdown of Requirements

Clinical Pastoral Education is a long-distance training program offered by the Association of Clinical Pastor Education (ACPE) and the Institute of Clinical Pastoral Training (ICPT). I strongly recommend ICPT because I went through this program and know several of the competent supervisors. ICPT is a tremendous organization. I cannot speak for the other, but it is another option for training.

With ICPT, each of the four units is 12 weeks. Therefore, it takes about a year to complete. You will be required to submit six case studies for peer review within the twelve weeks. The peer group will include four to eight trainees. They are usually experienced chaplains or new chaplains. However, the classes are not limited to these vocations. Each trainee will be responsible for reflective essays and a book review.

Every course requires a mid and final evaluation. Four hundred hours of training are also required to complete the unit. These hours are broken down into 300 hours of clinical on-the-job interaction and 100 hours of course work, which includes time spent on case studies, book reviews, reflections, etc. The on-the-job training can be done by volunteering in a local church, hospital or hospice agency. The supervisor of the on-the-job training is responsible for signing off on all case studies.

Descriptions of Presentations
Trainees are Required to Make

All trainees are required to share presentations, which are done in closed sessions utilizing Zoom or GoToMeeting technology setup. Your peer group will be on-screen, which enables interaction with them. The supervisor will have personal access with each trainee for private, as well as group sessions. The following subjects will be presented:

A. **Case Studies** The case studies contain several parts or sections. Each section will be under the scrutiny of your peers. Here is the basic outline of a case study and a brief explanation. The outline was created by a CPE Supervisor with ICPT. The explanations and comments are mine:

1. **Known Facts**: This is the known background of the patient or person interviewed or counseled.

2. **Preparation:** How the chaplain prepared for the visit or interview; reason for the visit

3. **Observation**: What was the chaplain's first impression: the setting, who were the other persons there?

B. **The Visit:** This is a very important part of the record. It is the verbatim account of verbal interaction with the patient. All individuals participating in the visit are assigned an identifying letter for their names with a number for each comment or action that takes place during the interview. Example: Chaplain: C:1, Patient: P:1, and Daughter: D:1

C: 1 Good morning, I'm Chaplain John.

D: 1 Good morning, Chaplain. Thank you for coming today.

P: 1 (Patient was eating her meal and responded with a smile and affirmative nod.)

The preceding is a record of what was said, who said it, the patient's reaction to the question asked, what emotions were expressed by the patient or how the chaplain felt. The focus of the visit was to gather information about the patient, but more importantly, to listen actively and use reflective statements like, "*I see you are angry.*" or "*I see having that experience hurt you,*" which requires a response by the patient. This part of the case study requires your full attention and focus on the patient. Your ability to recall and write what you heard is very important. Also, let me forewarn you the verbatim will be under the intense scrutiny of your peers. Therefore, you should expect and be prepared for the following questions:

1. "*Why did you say that?*"

2. *"What were you feeling when she said that?"*

3. *"Why were you angry?"*

4. *"Why are you crying right now?"*

5. *"What does this have to do with your father?"*

6. *"Why are you running from the room; we're having a meeting here."*

After thorough questioning, the supervisor may say: *"Wow! Now, we're making progress with John. Who wants to share their case study next?"*

I just described a typical case study review, which may cause you to introspect and ask yourself a pertinent question: "Do I still want to be a chaplain?" Of course! The next part of the case study is the analysis of the patient.

C. **The Analysis of the Patient:** This section should address various dynamics that may happen between the patient and the chaplain. This would include the conversation and change of topics or tone of voice during the visits. The chaplain will need to note any difficulties that may have occurred.

A. **Interpersonal Dynamics:** How does the patient relate to you, the family or the facility staff?

B. Intrapersonal Dynamics: What emotions were expressed? What was the patient's cognitive ability to understand the situation?

C. Theological/Philosophical Concerns: What is the patient's religious background? Is there any reality to the words and actions congruent with the stated religious background? Do the patient's walk and talk line up?

D. The Analysis of the Chaplain: (see above explanation)

1. **Interpersonal Dynamics:** The chaplain describes how he related to the patient, if there were any difficulties in communication, likes or dislikes about the patient. (Be ready to thoroughly explain anything written here.)

2. **Intrapersonal Dynamics:** In this section, the chaplain records how he felt the visit went. Did he accomplish his goals? Did he respond as a chaplain?

3. **Theological/Philosophical Concerns:** How did the chaplain respond to the patient's different religious views? How did he feel internally about a different religious view other than his/hers?

E. Next Steps: How will the chaplain follow up with the patient, future visits; describe a plan of action and why.

In my opinion, the case studies and peer reviews are the nuts and bolts of the entire CPE experience. I say *experience* because it is not something we will *do* and check off our list. Rather, it will be an *experience* of self-discovery that will be life-changing for the chaplain. Through my case studies and interaction with my peers, I discovered I talked too much. I was an interrupter, and I didn't listen very well. To my surprise, my wife Kathy said, "I could have told you that." She celebrated the change. I'm sure everybody else around me welcomed it as well — especially my patients.

The CPE course is about self-discovery and self-knowledge. Henry J. M. Nouwen called it *"the broken learning to heal the broken"* (Nouwen 88). There is no way to prepare for this experience apart from *knowing* it will happen to the student. I will recommend some must-read books to help you understand the CPE process: *Out of the Darkness,* by Aton T. Boisen. Aton Boisen is credited with being the founder of Clinical Pastoral Education. All his studies and discoveries were not in the classroom of the seminary, but rather studying what he called "the human document," which was the patient. Boisen said, *"It's not what the minister says to the boy. It is what the boy says to the minister."*

This book is out of print, but it can probably be found on Google Books or with rare books sellers. It is a very difficult book to read and understand. However, it does give some insight into the history and people involved in the beginning. Without this man's contribution, we probably wouldn't have a CPE program today. I think it should be required reading by all CPE students. Additionally, Rev. Glen H. Asquith, Jr. offers great insights on Boisen's work and research in *"The Case Study Method of Anton T. Boisen."*

In addition to Boisen's book, you can also use *"Recovery of Soul-A History and Memoir of the Clinical Pastoral Movement"* by Raymond J. Lawrence. *"The author provides an unvarnished account of the movement that revolutionized hospital chaplaincy and pastoral counseling over the last century."*[1]

I hope all the information I've shared thus far has been helpful. I want to continue to address the class work of CPE that will be required, and then I'll make some additional recommendations.

F. **Required Responses:** Each student will be required to make three responses to the case studies of each peer.

G. **Weekly Reflection:** The weekly reflection is written communication between the student and his/her supervisor. This is an opportune time to write a couple of paragraphs on any concerns or challenges the student may be going through. The supervisor may choose to have a face-to-face chat with the student via Zoom conference.

H. **Mid-Unit & Final Evaluation:** This evaluation will be concerned with the student's interaction and comments about his peer group, as well as the supervisor's assessment and teaching style. The final evaluation will be similar to the mid-unit, with an assessment of improvements in all areas.

I. **Weekly Supervision:** The student will meet weekly with the supervisor, primarily to assess previous goals set by the supervisor, as well as the student's personal goals for CPE.

J. **Book Reviews:** The supervisor of each group will select at least two books. The student will be required to write an overview of the books' principle topics. The supervisor will discuss each book review with the peer group.

In this section, I have endeavored to share the basics of the CPE training, in hopes of acquainting the student with general information that will encourage a successful completion.

Credentials

K. Ecclesiastical Endorsement

It is very important for a new chaplain or young minister to be credentialed with a recognized organization. *"Credentials often serve as an important way for chaplains to 'prove their professionalism to institutional employers and constituents'"* (Paget & McCormack121). Paul exhorted Timothy to *"Know them that labor among you,"* (I Thessalonians 5:13, NIV). He also mentioned that *"Those that shall hold positions should first be tested."*

In most cases, the chaplain is required to be ordained by an ecclesiastical 501c3 faith group and have pastoral experience. I also recommend the new chaplain to have memberships in other professional organizations. I have found two exceptional organizations: HealthCare Chaplaincy and the Spiritual

Care Association of Certified Christian Chaplains. These two organizations offer beneficial opportunities for continued education, as well as weekly emails on current events and changes in healthcare. Keep in mind that continuing education is also a requirement for annual re-certification of board-certified chaplains.

A note of encouragement to the new chaplain or minister regarding the availability of associate-level credentials: certification is available as Board-Certified Chaplain/ Associate or Board-Certified Pastoral Counselor.

1. **Board-Certified Chaplain (BCC)** is a professional who is employed in health care, prisons, military, etc.

2. **Board-Certified Pastoral Counselor (BCPC)** is, in most cases, a local church pastor with a primary responsibility to their congregation.

3. **Board-Certified Associate Chaplain (BCAC):** This category is for the chaplain who is seeking full board certification but has not completed (4) units of CPE or his/her bachelor's degree. Once the chaplain has completed the Master of Divinity, he/she is granted full board certification.

4. **Certified Chaplain Assistant (CCA)** is for those who have not acquired the higher education requirements as mentioned above. However, a high school diploma with some college credit is required. Application for all levels of certification can be made online at

certifiedchaplains.org.

L. **Checklist for Board Certification with the Association of Certified Christian Chaplains (APCC) — Website: *http://certifiedchaplains.org*:**

1. Documentation of existing CPE Units (not needed if the units were taken under ICPT or APCC)

2. Documentation of existing certifications(s) (if applying for reciprocation)

3. An ecclesiastical endorsement from your church body attesting to your suitability for chaplaincy or pastoral counseling (may be waived if the church body does not issue endorsements)

4. Evidence of a Master of Divinity degree or equivalent (equivalency is determined by the ACCC National Board)

5. Evidence of ordination, consecration or licensing by a recognized church body

6. A theological reflection (2-5 pages) that demonstrates your thoughts on chaplaincy or pastoral counseling in light of your faith

7. Two (2) recent case studies

8. A signed Affirmation of Faith (part of the application)

9. A brief autobiography (no more than 2 pages) outlining your journey through faith.

Notes:

1. Lawrence, Raymond J. *Recovery of Soul – A History and Memoir of the Clinical Pastoral Movement*, Cover Quote.

Chapter Seven
A Typical Day in the Life of a Chaplain

Quiet time, patient visits, charting, end-of-day reports and route sheets are all part of a chaplain's day. For this hospice chaplain, it means I usually start around 4:00 a.m. Sometimes at 3:00 a.m. I quietly go downstairs to start my devotions. The earlier risings are on days when I feel the need for more preparation.

My time alone with God in the early hours is precious to me before the busyness of life begins. I would not endeavor to walk this path of ministry without this infusion of spiritual strength and divine direction for the day. During this quiet time, on many occasions, I have been directed to visit certain patients immediately rather than the next scheduled time — just hours before their departure into eternity.

These hours of devotion include Bible reading, a variety of devotion books, prayer time with my wife, and a time of sharing together for the coming day. We agree in prayer together. We laugh together. We make decisions together that affect our paths for the day, our family, and our future.

Prayer is a key part of our daily lives. Dick Eastman quotes S.D. Gordon saying, *"The great people of the earth today are the people who pray. I do not mean those who talk about prayer; nor those who say they believe in prayer; nor yet those who can explain about prayer; but I mean these people who take time to pray."*[1]

Prayer must be a central part of our morning devotions and quiet time. Proverbs 31:8 admonishes, *"Speak up for those who cannot speak for themselves"* (NIV). Isaiah 50:4 states, *"To know the word that sustains the weary...wakens me morning by morning, wakens my ear, to listen like one being taught"* (NIV). If we don't pray for our patients, who will?

I challenge you as a new chaplain to develop a deep intimacy with God, as well, in order to be led by the Spirit of God in each situation. In E. M. Bounds' book, he states the following: *"We must first talk to God about men before we talk to men about God."*[2]

Also, there must be occasions when the chaplain experiences deep communication with God beyond the daily reading of the Bible. He or she must develop an ongoing relationship with God in worship. This can easily begin with a personal time of worship using CDs in the private devotions, and during a busy day in the car between visits. Worship is the only thing that can heal a broken or troubled heart. How can we expect to bring life and encouragement to hurting people unless we have been in the presence of God and heard His voice in our spirits? *"Call unto me and I will answer you and tell you great and unsearchable things you do not know"* (Jeremiah 33:3, NIV). *"My sheep know my voice"* (John 10:27, NIV). With that anointing, we have the confidence to pray in faith, speak words of encouragement in faith, and see God work mightily in our daily lives.

Normally, I start work at 7:00 a.m. By that, I mean I go to my computer and finish any charting left over from the day before or other paperwork such as the end-of-day report and route sheets. If these have been completed, then I read emails and texts received through the night to check on the status of my patients. The information I receive from these updates may change my proposed schedule of visits for the day.

I am usually out of the house and on the road by 7:30 or 8:00 a.m. at the latest. I plan to visit at least a minimum of five patients each day. If they are all in different facilities that require a lot of driving, that can be challenging.

Most days are filled with patient visits. I covered some of this information in a previous chapter regarding the initial and routine patient visits. However, I would like to share a few more specific details. Hospice ministry visits are similar, yet, different in many ways from what a pastor or young minister may have experienced. Hospice patients are, in most cases, located in retirement communities, assisted-living facilities, board and care facilities and homes, rather than hospitals. The chaplain has to keep in mind that all assigned patients are required to be visited each month or he/she would be out of compliance, which adds a little more stress to your day.

The hospice patient comes to our team with a six months or less prognosis. In some cases, only weeks to a few days are given to the patient, where the average hospital stay is one to three days maximum. Many hospice patients are non-verbal, and generally, half of our patients have dementia or Alzheimer's at varying stages, which presents unique challenges to ongoing communication.

The initial visit, like the name suggests, is the introductive visit to meet the patient and the family.

The patient is admitted into hospice usually from the hospital or a retirement community, etc.

Our policy at Sonata is (when schedules permit) to make a team introduction. We do this in an effort not to overwhelm the patient with five different visits by each of the team members (nurse, social worker, music therapist, home health person, and the chaplain). The admission can be an emotional situation in itself, so adding several separate visits from team members can be very stressful for the patient and family.

Again, the initial visit is an assessment of the patient's health and emotional well-being. It is made, in a general sense, with a family member, if present. Basically, this is a fact-finding interview. There are a lot of questions asked by each team member to determine a baseline for the plan of care going forward. For the chaplain, this is a time for short questions and reflective listening.

Reflective listening takes place when the chaplain takes the time to not only acquire information but also to try to understand the feelings of the patient, for his or her sake. To do that, the chaplain must develop an attitude of "*taking a walk*" with the person. As a chaplain, if the patients are alert and verbal, I ask them to tell me their story (life review). If not, I ask a family member. In doing so, I offer reflective listening for emotional words

67

like *"That hurt me." "That was a difficult time."* Or *"I cried when..."* etc. I walk with them on their journey.

My usual responses are: *"Please, tell me more." "You feel ..." "As I hear it, you ..." "Sort of feeling ..."* This type of listening requires your focused attention. It is *"listening with your face,"* a term I previously mentioned that was in our family for years. In other words, I need you to focus on me, look at me, and *listen* to what I am trying to convey to you. Another term to know and to use is *"Lean into the patient."* This gives you a better listening advantage and conveys to the person talking, you are listening. Hearing all the facts makes it easier to give objective feedback, summarize the events, and ask the right questions. This assures the patient you are truly listening.

Next, the routine visit and its frequency have been determined in the plan of care for the spiritual needs of the individual patient. Depending on the cognitive ability of the patient and his/her response to spiritual matters, I plan accordingly. However, if the patient is sleeping, I do not disturb him/her. I generally sit at the bedside and offer the ministry of presence.

I first encountered the term "ministry of presence" in Clinical Pastoral Education courses, and it has proven to be very valuable in my ministry as a hospice chaplain. I realized that many times, great comfort is given to an individual by the chaplain's calm stability. Just "being" with the patient, with little or few words, can cause their fears to subside. I remember receiving a call from a young man that his grandmother had just passed in the hospital. Arriving at the hospital room, I found him with his wife and father at the bedside. I offered my condolences with words of comfort and a prayer of blessing. I took a seat nearby and chose not to speak but to offer the ministry of presence. Later, the family mentioned how thankful they were to me for *"just being there."* They added, *"We don't think we could have gotten through it without you there."* Presence speaks volumes of comfort to those in need.

It is amazing how the Holy Spirit directs the chaplain through his day. Normally, on a typical day, the office will add one or two new "admits" to my schedule. This will add one to two hours to my day as I meet the new patient and determine what kind of care he/she requires – or in some cases refuses. When this occurs, I have to reschedule patients I had intended to visit that day. It is company policy to stop for lunch after four hours and no later than five hours. The last two hours of the day are used to handle the administrative side of hospice ministry. After a busy day of visiting patients, we have to document our day (charting, end of day report and route sheet). These reports are equally important to complete by the end of the day.

Charting is officially called the Electronic Medical Record (EMR). The chaplain is responsible for adding his/her visit narratives to the patient's medical record, (EMR), which is contained in his/her tablet. All disciplines – doctors, nurses, social workers, chaplains, etc. – must record their interactions with patients that day. This is labor- intensive and time-consuming. Just as a reminder, all entries become legal documents; therefore, accuracy is imperative. For example, "The patient appeared to be asleep." That statement would not be considered accurate. Rather, the chaplain should report that "The patient did not respond to greetings or a gentle touch." That answer is more definitive and would be considered accurate by a Joint Commission surveyor. Also, regarding time references, the chaplain must report exact times – not "It was around 4 o'clock," but rather, "It was 4:12 p.m." The chaplain must also report with the same exactness the patient's condition upon arrival and at the end of the visit. Charting can be challenging, to say the least.

The route sheet is your record of time spent traveling to your patients and with the patient. Time spent with the patient includes phone calls to family members or any other contact related to the patient's healthcare. This can be completed on a printed form or in Excel and forwarded to your designated office for their records.

The end of day report is a generally short overview of the patients visited: where, who you spoke to, and any other noteworthy information. This information is emailed to all staff members to read and consider. One triage team scans all EODs, looking for patient issues like falls, family dynamics, discharges, patients actively dying, etc. to assess the challenges they may be facing and the after-hours services needed.

This concludes a "typical day" of eight hours, and I normally return home between 5:00 and 6:00 p.m.

Notes:

1. Eastman, Dick *No Easy Road* p 16.

2. Bounds, E. M. *The Complete Work of E. M. Bounds* p 332.

Chapter Eight
Special Days

Special days and meetings have to be fitted into a chaplain's already busy schedule. There are monthly staff meetings, weekly Inter-Disciplinary Team (IDT) meetings, conference calls, Safety & Infection Control meetings, and Quality Assessment meetings, and not to forget, the occasional impromptu meetings. If the chaplain is not careful, he/she could easily get frustrated with the interruptions, having 40 to 50 patients to visit each month to stay in compliance with the government regulations. However, patience and flexibility are two virtues that must be embraced.

Monthly staff meetings are held on the first Friday of each month. These usually involve a catered lunch of some type and are used to build camaraderie, hand out awards, and make announcements. New staff members are introduced as well.

Conference calls can be difficult to work into the daily schedule; however, they are preferred to the interruption of driving to the office and sitting in a meeting that may or may not relate to the field of the chaplain. A lot of staff training is dealt with in this way to stay in compliance. At times, part of the conference call is delegated to the chaplain to bring a report or point of view.

Out of all the special days the chaplain has to schedule throughout the month, the IDT meeting takes priority. Everything is scheduled around this major event each week, including patient visits. Only by a total group effort and hours of preparation does this become a successful happening.

The Inter-Disciplinary Team consists of the following team members:

- Doctor – Medical Director of our hospice

- Patient Care Nurses

- Social Workers

- Bereavement Coordinator

- Music Therapist

- All the RNs, which could be at least four to five

- The Chaplain (of course)

This four-hour meeting includes the recognition of patients who recently passed, the discussion of patients who are being evaluated, and those who may be discharged from hospice care. About 75 patients' health conditions are discussed and reviewed in detail primarily by the doctor and the nurses with supporting information offered by team members. This four-hour meeting contains moments that are very somber, stressful, and sad, as well as times of levity, laughter, and sharing personal experiences with our patients.

Chapter Nine
Office Dynamics

Over the years, many things have changed in the workplace. Today, we have sensitivity training for interaction with the LGBTQ community. In California, we have shared restrooms. At our office, the same key opens either male or female restrooms. It is your choice.

In light of these changes, I feel an even greater responsibility to exemplify respectful conduct above reproach. To present this professional standard to the ministry of the chaplain, and, more importantly, the office of a spiritual advisor ordained by God, I will share some of the personal rules of conduct I adhere to. I have observed other staff members who did not follow these standards. Ultimately, they were removed by the company or resigned due to personal reasons. I am not saying the lack of any one or all of these recommendations caused their exits. I will say attitudes cannot be hidden for long, and eventually, the inward state of the heart is revealed.

Attitudes of the Heart and Coarse Language in the Workplace

First and foremost, I will address language. A very important scripture, and one that gives clear insight into the heart of a man, is found in Matthew 6:45, KJV: *"A good man out of the good treasure of his heart brings forth good; and an evil man out of the evil treasure of his heart brings forth evil. For out of the abundance of the heart his mouth speaks."*

Coarse language is a fruit of the attitude of the heart. A hospice agency is not a church organization. It is not a spiritual organization, even though they hire chaplains to provide a needed and desired service to the patients. Most of the employees of the hospice agency have hearts to serve or they would not be in this chosen field. However, it is a secular world with many different faiths represented and several belief systems in play. Moral values are different. The language in the workplace can be very coarse and not befitting for a chaplain to participate in. One can be lighthearted and witty to bring levity to the team. However, language elevates or diminishes the level of perceived authority and rightly so.

Attitudes of the heart are easily discerned by simply listening to the words spoken. I tend to live by this rule: "Challenges up – praises down." I taught this rule to my church leadership for years and follow it now in the corporate world. I refuse to listen to disgruntled team members. Instead, I always encourage them to speak directly to their supervisors, thus "challenges up." Praise and encouragement are liberally bestowed on fellow team members – "praises down." I always encourage others to follow the will of God in their lives. God *"determines the exact places where we live"* (Acts 17:26, NIV). One of the keys to fulfillment I have embraced is, *"Never demean; always esteem."*[1]

Practically speaking, I always leave the door slightly open if I am in a meeting with a female co-worker. I have learned in the corporate world to never hug. This was difficult for me, coming from a pastoral ministry of over forty years where hugs were common. However, we live in a different culture today. Physical touch should be avoided. I only go to lunch with co-workers in groups. If a counseling session is requested or needed, I invite my wife or another chaplain to come along.

I will now list, more succinctly, seven areas I feel are most important in this section of staff dynamic principles. My wife and I personally live by these. They have been learned through many years of counseling and working with people in several different forums – church boards, church staff, national and international ministries, the corporate world of legal offices, and now hospice organizations. These principles were developed, learned or observed from many personal life experiences.

The Don'ts of Staff Dynamics

a. **Don't touch any woman except your mother.** Don't touch a man except your father. If spiritual powers want to destroy a minister and his ministry, he uses a person. Guard yourself. Use the open door – in plain sight policy – when meeting with the opposite sex.

b. **Don't share political views with others in the workplace.** Having an opinion and sharing it are two different things. In the staff dynamics, political views polarize people and create the "them and us" groups. This is very unhealthy and destroys synergy among the team members. If I am ever drawn into a political conversation, my standard answer is, "I am sorry; I don't watch the news very much, and I'm not sure what you are talking about." This is a true statement because we don't watch the constant negative news. We use other resources to keep up with national and world events.

c. **We don't talk to anybody about anything!** As pastors, we found that certain people were always "fishing" for information about the pastor and the pastor's family. In light of this, we taught our two girls this principle in a phrase they could easily remember. I highly recommend the same for employers and employees. The "fishermen" live in abundance among staff. Don't be a listening ear and a gatherer of information. The best answer is, "I'm sorry. I don't talk to anybody about anything, so you're talking to the wrong person." Don't receive and pass along anything.

d. **We don't write anything we don't want read back to us in court.** This would be comments in emails, social media, and Electronic Medical Records, i.e. charting. Everything written can be audited or subpoenaed.

e. **Don't discuss matters with peers in the hearing of "smart assistant-powered devices."** It may send them an email or text including your comments, which actually happened – Google the lawsuits. This reminds me of the admonishment by King Solomon, *"Do not revile the king even in your thoughts or curse the rich in your bedroom, because a bird of the air may carry your words, and a bird on the wing may report what you say"* (Ecclesiastes 10:20, NIV).

f. **We don't discuss problems with anyone who cannot resolve them.** We use the chain of authority. In the military, it is called the chain of command. The principle is – always discuss problems with the person who has the authority to effect change. As a manager of people, we give encouragement and praise to those we are directing. Again, the principle in simple terms is "challenges up and praises down."

g. **We never ever disrespect people, especially in front of others.** A pastor friend taught me years ago, if I continually disrespect something, it will eventually leave my life. If I disrespect my health, I will lose it. If I disrespect my automobile, it breaks down. If I continually disrespect a person, that person will eventually leave my life.

Summary

As chaplains it goes without saying that we are "open epistles read by many" (2 Corinthians 3:32) and are to exemplify that lifestyle. If you make a mistake, apologize. Walk in humility and thankfulness that you are a part of a great team.

Notes:

1. Osborn, T. L. and Daisy *You Are God's Best* p105.

Chapter Ten
"On Call" Ministry

"On Call" is another aspect of a hospice agency that I consider crucial to chaplain ministry. This entails being available *after a normal workday of eight hours*. The "on call" duty starts at 5:00 p.m. in the afternoon until 8:00 a.m. the next morning (15 hours), Monday through Friday – plus, 24 hours on Saturday and Sunday, ending Monday morning at 8:00 a.m. Typically, the calls received during these times are for patients who are imminent or passing. Office policy requires those "on call" to be available within twenty minutes of the call and be en route to the facility or home.

At times, if a patient is imminent, the family members panic. They call for a chaplain to help them through the difficult hours. Sometimes, a phone call will calm the family member. At other times, it may require a visit to the home or facility. If the visit is prior to the patient passing, I always encourage the family and friends to share with the patients and include three things:

1. How much they love and care for them

2. How their lives made a difference to them

3. That the patient will be remembered for the specific impact on their lives

At times, the team member on call may be asked to sit with a patient. On occasion, as a chaplain, you are the only one to offer continuous care. This could be if the patient is suicidal or a fall risk. It could also include patients who have no family, friends, or anyone except the chaplain or whoever is available on staff. It is our agency's policy that no one dies alone. Our hospice team members sit at the patient's bedside and offer the ministry of presence and comfort during their last hours. The on call chaplain is usually assigned to handle this type of service/ministry. These are wonderful opportunities for ministry. We are privileged to spend the last remaining minutes with the patient before he/she enters eternity. As chaplains, we bring peace and assurance that are only there because the Holy Spirit is ministering through us to the patient and family.

One last thought regarding on call ministry - as you know, personal schedules get full, family dynamics occur, and unplanned events happen. Team members may be unavailable for their shifts for any number of reasons. My personal work ethic is to always be available to do what others can't or are unwilling to do. However, there are self-care limits to everything. Use wisdom.

Chapter Eleven
The Death Visit

In my opinion, the death visit is probably the most challenging part of the job. Yet, it can be the most fulfilling part of the chaplain's ministry. I had only been on staff for a few days when I experienced my first death visit. I don't recall the lead chaplain giving me any special instructions, apart from the fact that we were going on this particular visit to assist the family. I sat with the family member offering condolences, spiritual conversation, and comfort, while the lead chaplain handled all the phone calls and mortuary arrangements. When the mortuary personnel arrived, I also had to assist the pickup agent with body preparation and moving the deceased patient through narrow doorways, halls, and down a flight of stairs to the van. It was physically challenging at times, but everything went smoothly.

It turns out this visit had been a test to challenge my emotional response and ability to minister to the family. The lead chaplain mentioned to me as we left the home that I had passed the test. Test? I didn't know a test was going on. I thought it was a prime opportunity for ministry. Interestingly enough, three years later, that same family member came on hospice service as my patient, and I was able to lead him to the Lord before he passed. Thank God for His grace and mercy in all things.

As chaplains, we comfort the grieving family and help them walk through this very emotional time in their lives. As briefly mentioned, there will be a lot of details that will have to be addressed during the visit; however, the initial concern is comforting the family. Assuming all the family members have been notified and they are grieving appropriately, the chaplain will need to receive permission from the family to contact the mortuary. At that point, the administrative part of the death visit can begin.

The call to the mortuary is the first and most important phone call to be made by the chaplain. The reason is that California laws only allow the deceased to remain in the facility for four hours from the time of death (TOD). The normal estimated time of pickup is a minimum of 90 minutes to two hours. When you add that time into when the patient passed, the on-time arrival by the mortuary becomes critical. The laws are different and more complicated regarding death at home, so I will only address the facility situation at this time.

The mortuary drivers are not always available or have trouble finding the facility, especially homes or apartments. It is a good practice for the chaplain to give his cell number to the driver so he/she can be updated on arrival time or any changes in schedule. These visits tend to extend from two to five hours depending on the number of family members present and the efficiency of the mortuary company driver. However, during this waiting period, the chaplain makes all the calls, texts, and emails to everyone involved in the healthcare of the deceased patient. This includes doctors, nurses, ministry teams, etc.

The arrival of the mortuary driver may create another emotional moment for the grieving family. Although it is not required, as a chaplain, I generally stay through this event to support the family. If the deceased is a veteran, I offer a flag ceremony upon his/her departure from the facility or home. Our hospice has a bereavement department that offers grief support for the family for over a year.

In hospice ministry, all patients are in the process of dying. Patients are not on hospice service unless their prognosis is less than six months to live. Someone asked me one day how many of my patients die. I regrettably said, "All of them." The Sonata team ministered to 400 to 500 people this last year.

As a hospice chaplain, I deal with death and dying on a daily or weekly basis. We have been given the unique gift to *"comfort them that mourn"* and bring a calm assurance to the dying. Sometimes our theology does not line up with the acts of our mighty God. When our mercy for others ends, God's grace continues on and on. We are on this incredible journey called life. We have been given the opportunity as chaplains to share the last moments of people's lives. They may have lived 97 years and only experienced God during the last few moments while we are at their bedside. Sometimes, we will hold their hands as they step into eternity. Ours are the last human voices they hear "as though God was making His appeal through us" (2 Corinthians 5:20). So we endeavor to stay sensitive to the Holy Spirit.

It is a great honor to serve in this way. God has brought some unique people across my path. It's marvelous how they have impacted my life and hopefully, in some small way, our hospice team has impacted theirs. This is truly a holy journey not all get to take or for that matter, want to take. It is only for those of us who have been called by our wonderful Lord and Savior.

Conclusion

As I mentioned, we are all on this incredible journey called life. Pastor Rick Warren writes as an opening statement in his book, *The Purpose Driven Life*, "It's not about you. It's about God."[1] He goes on to ask throughout the book, in my words: what are we asking God to reveal about His will for us and our contribution to this life?

Not everyone can do hospice ministry, but those of us who *can* have been uniquely gifted by our gracious and loving God to make a contribution to the lives of those who are nearing the end of theirs. Someone made a statement years ago that challenges us all today: *"Always be a part of something bigger than yourself."*[2] I found this challenge as a hospice chaplain. As I endeavor to walk the final days and hours of patients' lives with them and their families, this difficult journey requires more than self can give. It requires divine enablement. My prayer for you as you enter this area of ministry is that you, too, will find incredible fulfillment in God's will and call upon your life.

Notes:

1. Warren, Rick *Purpose Driven* Life p17.

2. Author Unknown.

One final thought ...

If you have purchased this book on Amazon and it makes a difference in your life, please consider writing a review to encourage others in their search for answers.

Bibliography

The Amplified Bible, Expanded Edition, The Zondervan Corporation and The Lockman Foundation 1987

Boisen, Anton T. Out of Darkness. New York: Harper and Brothers, 1960

Boulay, Shirley du. Updated by Rankin, Marianne. Cicely Saunders: The Founder of the Modern Hospice Movement. London: Hodder & Stoughton, 2007

Bounds, E. M. The Complete Works of E. M. Bounds. Grand Rapids: Baker House 1990

Crabb, Lawrence Dibasic Principles of Biblical Counseling. Grand Rapids: Zondervan 1975

Crane, William E. Where God Comes In: The Divine "Plus" in Counseling. Waco - London: Word Books 1970

Eastman, Dick. No Easy Road. Grand Rapids: Baker House 1971

Karnes, Barbara. The Final Act of Living. Vancouver: Barbara Karnes Books, Inc. 2012

Kessler, David. The Needs of the Dying: A Guide for Bringing Hope, Comfort and Love to Life's Final Chapter. New York: Harper Collins Books 2007

Health Care Chaplaincy Network, Spiritual Care: What It Means, Why It Matters In Health Care. October 2016

Holst, Lawrence E. Hospital Ministry: The Role of the Chaplain Today. New York: The Crossroad Publishing Company 1996

Lawrence, Raymond J. Recovery of the Soul A History and Memoir of the Clinical Pastoral Movement. New York: CPSP Press, 2017.

Nouwen, Henry J. M., The Wounded Healer. New York: Doubleday, 1979

Osborn, T.L. and Daisy. You Are God's Best. Tulsa: Osborn Ministries 1984

Paget, Naomi K. and McCormack, Janet, R. The Work of the Chaplain. Valley Forge: Judson Press 2006

Peck, M. Scott, M.D. The Road Less Traveled: A New Psychology of Love, Traditional Values and Spiritual Growth. New York: Simon and Schuster 1978

The NIV/KJV Parallel Bible, The Zondervan Corporation 1983

The New King James Version Bible, Thomas Nelson 1982

Stoddard, Sandol. The Hospice Movement: A Better Way of Caring for the Dying. Briarcliff Manor: Stein and Day 1978

The Thompson Chain-Reference New International Version, Compiled and Edited by Frank Charles Thompson, D.D.Ph.D., Co-Published by The B.B. Kirkbride Bible Company, Inc. and the Zondervan Corporation 1983

Warren, Rick. Purpose Driven Life. Grand Rapids: Zondervan 2002

Wilkerson, Bruce H. The 7 Laws of the Learner: Textbook Addition. Sisters: Multnomah Publishers 1992

Additional Reading

Cicely Saunders-The Founder of the Modern Hospice Movement - Shirley du Boulay & Marianne Rankin

Crisis & Trauma Counseling-A Practical Guide for Ministers, Counselors and Lay Counselors - Dr. H. Norman Wright

Gone From My Sight The Dying Experience – Barbara Karnes, RN

Grief Recovery Handbook-The Action Program for Moving Beyond Death, Divorce, and Other Losses – John W. James and Russell Friedman

Man's Search for Meaning -Viktor E. Frankl

On Death And Dying-What The Dying Have To Teach Doctors, Nurses, Clergy, And Their Own Families - Elisabeth Kubler-Ross, M.D.

On Grief and Grieving-Finding the Meaning of Grief Through the Five Stages of Loss – Elisabeth Kubler-Ross and David Kessler

***

Caring for the Human Spirit Magazine – Great articles (subscription -first copy free)

Health Care Chaplaincy Network

(www.healthcharechaplaincy.org)

SpiritualCareAssociation.org

The Chaplain Connection-Spiritual Care Tips of the Day

Association of Certified Christian Chaplains

certifiedchaplains.org

Made in the USA
Coppell, TX
30 August 2025

54093715R00066